40
DAYS
— of —
FAITH

Books by Paul David Tripp

40
DAYS

—of—

FAITH

PAUL DAVID TRIPP

WHEATON, ILLINOIS

40 Days of Faith

Copyright © 2020 by Paul David Tripp

Published by Crossway
   1300 Crescent Street
   Wheaton, Illinois 60187

The devotions in this book appeared previously in Paul David Tripp, *New Morning Mercies: A Daily Gospel Devotional* (Wheaton, IL: Crossway, 2014).

Cover design: Josh Dennis

First printing, 2020

Printed in the United States of America

Trade paperback ISBN: 978-1-4335-7425-2
ePub ISBN: 978-1-4335-7428-3
PDF ISBN: 978-1-4335-7426-9
Mobipocket ISBN: 978-1-4335-7427-6

Library of Congress Cataloging-in-Publication Data

Names: Tripp, Paul David, 1950– author.
Title: 40 days of faith / Paul David Tripp.
Other titles: Forty days of faith
Description: Wheaton, Illinois: Crossway, 2020. | "The devotions in this book
 appeared previously in Paul David Tripp, New Morning Mercies: A Daily Gospel
 Devotional(Wheaton, IL: Crossway, 2014)."
Identifiers: LCCN 2020022785 (print) | LCCN 2020022786 (ebook) | ISBN
 9781433574252 (trade paperback) | ISBN 9781433574269 (pdf) | ISBN
 9781433574276 (mobipocket) | ISBN 9781433574283 (epub)
Subjects: LCSH: Trust in God—Christianity—Meditations. | Faith—Meditations.
Classification: LCC BV4637 .T75 2020 (print) | LCC BV4637 (ebook) | DDC
 242/.2—dc23
LC record available at https://lccn.loc.gov/2020022785
LC ebook record available at https://lccn.loc.gov/2020022786

Crossway is a publishing ministry of Good News Publishers.

LB		28	27	26	25	24	23	22	21	20
14	13	12	11	10	9	8	7	6	5	4	3	2	1

INTRODUCTION

FAITH IS AT ONCE A VERY IMPORTANT and very confusing word.
I once tried to get a definition of faith out of a small group
of people I was speaking to. We walked a circle of synonyms
that led us back to the original word—*belief, trust, faith*. As
we arrived back where we began, it hit me that these people
heard and used this word all the time, but didn't understand
it. The word *faith* was in the Bible that they read, in the songs
of worship that they sang, and in the sermons that they heard,
but it still wasn't clear to them. Yet God, in his word, gives it
an extremely high level of importance.

Habakkuk 2:4 says, "The righteous shall live by his faith."
Just as you cannot physically live without breathing oxygen,
you cannot spiritually live without exercising faith. Faith is
breathing in the oxygen of God's grace, giving life to my once-
dead heart. What could be more important than that? Hebrews
11:6 says, "And without faith it is impossible to please him"
(God). You and I will never be what we were designed to be
and live as we have been called to live without faith. It is faith
that propels us to live in a way that is pleasing to the Lord.
What could be more important than this?

Here is why faith is so essential in God's redemptive plan.
Sin has rendered us incapable of pleasing God on our own. On

our best day, with our best intentions and exercising our best efforts, we fall horribly short of God's holy and wise standard. We can't even keep our own laws, let alone his. That is why God sent his Son. Jesus measured up to God's standard in all the ways that we are unable to and he paid our penalty with his own life. So God doesn't ask us to perfectly obey his law in order to please him. No, what God asks of us is this one simple thing: faith.

Faith is more than intellectual assent to God's existence. It is more than committing yourself to a community of faith and a regular set of religious habits. Faith is more than developing biblical literacy and doctrinal knowledge. Faith is not saying, "I believe that," when it makes little difference in the way you think about yourself, the way you relate to God, and the way you live your life. Faith is something that shatters you and rebuilds you. Faith is a transaction of your heart that will radically alter the way you live your life.

Faith is abandoning your own righteousness and entrusting the hope of your soul, in this life and the one to come, to the righteousness of another. Faith is the willingness to confess, without excuse or shifting the blame, sins that you once denied or hid. Faith is abandoning your own wisdom and feeding your heart on the wisdom of God. Faith is giving up on your delusions of control and resting in God's sovereign authority. Faith is admitting your weakness and crying out for the strength that only God can give. Faith is refusing to be a glory thief any longer and living for the greater glory of God.

Faith is taking up your cross, dying to yourself, and committing yourself to live as a disciple of Jesus. Faith is letting the cross of Jesus Christ and his empty tomb define your identity and your hope. Faith is much more than a one-time decision; it is a lifestyle lived with the presence, promises, and call of God always in view.

I'm about to write something that will surprise you. Faith is impossible. It is unnatural and counterintuitive for us all. Self-trust is natural. Fear is natural. Worry is natural. Self-righteousness is natural. Doubt is natural. Autonomy and self-sufficiency are natural, but faith isn't natural. So here's where the call to faith always leads you. Faith, properly understood, always leads you to cry out for God's grace. It takes grace to have the faith to entrust yourself and everything you are and have to God and his grace. Faith is important because it is the only pathway to finding and receiving God's greatest gift, his grace in the person of his Son, Jesus.

So I am inviting you to take a forty-day faith journey with me. If you do, you will come to know Jesus better, you will celebrate his grace more fully, and things in your heart and life will become more pleasing to him. Remember, without faith it is simply impossible for anyone to please him.

DAY 1

*Faith in Christ is not just about knowing the truths
of the gospel, but about living them as well.*

IT IS VITAL TO KNOW that faith is not just an action of your brain; it's an investment of your life. Faith is not just something you think; it's something you live. Hear these words from Hebrews 11:

> Now faith is the assurance of things hoped for, the conviction of things not seen. For by it the people of old received their commendation. By faith we understand that the universe was created by the word of God, so that what is seen was not made out of things that are visible.
>
> By faith Abel offered to God a more acceptable sacrifice than Cain, through which he was commended as righteous, God commending him by accepting his gifts. And through his faith, though he died, he still speaks. By faith Enoch was taken up so that he should not see death, and he was not found, because God had taken him. Now before he was taken he was commended as having pleased God. And without faith it is impossible to please him, for whoever would draw near to God must believe that he exists and that he rewards those who seek him. By faith Noah, being warned by God concerning events as yet unseen, in reverent fear constructed an ark for the saving of his household. By this he condemned the world and became an heir of the righteousness that comes by faith. (vv. 1–7)

What is faith? Verse 6 is very helpful. Biblical faith has this foundation—you must believe that God exists. This is the watershed, the great divide. There are only two types of people in this world—those who believe that the most important fact that a human being could ever consider and give assent to is the existence of God, and those who either casually or philosophically deny his existence. But intellectual commitment to God's existence is not all that faith is about; faith means you live as though you believe in God's existence, or as though you believe, as the writer says, "he rewards those who seek him."

Faith is a deep-seated belief in the existence of God that radically alters the way you live your life. Now, here's the rub. Faith isn't natural for us. Biblical faith is counterintuitive and countercultural. So we even need God's grace to have faith to believe in the existence of the one whose grace we so desperately need. And the grace is yours for the asking again today.

FOR FURTHER STUDY AND ENCOURAGEMENT
James 2:14–26

DAY 2

God calls you to believe and then works with zeal to craft you into a person who really does live by faith.

I DON'T KNOW HOW MUCH you've thought about this, but faith isn't natural for you and me. Doubt is natural. Fear is natural. Living on the basis of your collected experience is natural. Pushing the current catalog of personal "what-ifs" through your mind before you go to sleep or when you wake up in the morning is natural. Living based on the thinking of your brain and your physical senses is natural. Envying the life of someone else and wondering why it isn't your life is natural. Wishing that you were more sovereign over people, situations, and locations than you will ever be is natural. Manipulating your way into personal control so you can guarantee that you will get what you think you need is natural. Looking horizontally for the peace that you will only ever find vertically is natural. Anxiously wishing for change in things that you have no ability to change is natural. Giving way to despondency, discouragement, depression, or despair is natural. Numbing yourself with busyness, material things, media, food, or some other substance is natural. Lowering your standards to deal with your disappointment is natural. But faith simply isn't natural to us.

So, in grace, God grants us to believe. As Paul says in Ephesians 2:8, faith really is the gift of God. There is no more counterintuitive function to the average, sin-damaged human being than faith in God. Sure, we'll put our faith in a lot of things, but not in a God we cannot see or hear, who makes promises so grand they seem impossible to keep. God gives us the power to first believe, but he doesn't stop there. By grace he works in the situations, locations, and relationships of our everyday lives to craft, hammer, bend, and mold us into people who build life based on the radical belief that he really does exist and he really does reward those who seek him (Heb. 11:6).

Next time you face the unexpected, a moment of difficulty you really don't want to go through, remember that such a moment doesn't picture a God who has forgotten you, but one who is near to you and doing in you a very good thing. He is rescuing you from thinking that you can live the life you were meant to live while relying on the inadequate resources of your wisdom, experience, righteousness, and strength; and he is transforming you into a person who lives a life shaped by radical God-centered faith. He is the ultimate craftsman, and we are his clay. He will not take us off his wheel until his fingers have molded us into those who really do believe and do not doubt.

FOR FURTHER STUDY AND ENCOURAGEMENT
Mark 6:30–52

DAY 3

As God's child, live today with the surety,
hope, and courage that come from knowing
that your standing before God is secure.

YOU WANT TO BE SURE. You want to be secure. You want to
have hope. You want to live with courage. You don't want to
be weakened by fear, paralyzed by doubt, or filled with the
anxiety of wondering what's next. You want to know that
your life means something. You want to know that your labors are worth something. You want to know that you're not
alone. You want to know that you'll have the resources to face
whatever is coming next. You want to have inner peace. You
want to have motivation to continue. You don't want to feel
unprepared, weak, or unable. You don't ever want to think
that it's all been for naught. Yes, you want to stand on the
firm foundation of surety, and you will look to something
to give it to you.

The fact of the matter is that in a world where things break,
die, get corrupted, or otherwise fade away, surety is found only
vertically. If you're God's child, your standing before him is
sure, and because it is, you have surety in life right here, right
now; in death; and in eternity:

- You have the surety of knowing that you don't have to
  hide or playact, because every one of your sins and weaknesses has been covered by Jesus's blood.

- You don't have to fear that you will not have what it takes, because your Savior gives you all that you need to do what he's called you to do.
- You don't have to worry that you'll be left alone, because your Savior has made you the place where he dwells.
- You don't have to live with regret, because all your past sins have been forgiven by his grace.
- You don't have to search for identity, meaning, or purpose, because he has made you his child and called you to his purpose.
- You don't have to worry about the future, because all the mysteries of what is to come are held in his sovereign hands.
- You don't have to fear trouble, difficulty, or suffering, because your Savior uses all these things for your good and his glory.
- You don't have to hope that your labors are worth something, because the work you do in his name is never in vain.
- You don't have to fear being punished, because your Savior took your punishment and satisfied God's anger.

Yes, by faith you stand before God sure and secure, and because you do, your life right now is blessed with every kind of security you could ever want.

FOR FURTHER STUDY AND ENCOURAGEMENT
Ephesians 1

DAY 4

*You're not called to work for God's acceptance; you're called
to trust the one who completed that work on your behalf.*

WE KEEP TRYING IT, even though we've been told again and
again that it's impossible. It causes us to be either delusionally
proud or irrationally fearful. It causes us to hide in guilt and
shame, fearing the only one who can help us. In fear, we work
for what we have already been given. In weakening hope, we
seek what we already have. In redemptive delusion, some of
us boast about what we did not earn or achieve on our own.
In our misunderstanding, we envy what we think others have
and we wish we could achieve what they have accomplished.
We spend our lives feeling not only that we haven't measured
up, but also that we'll never measure up. We wonder what God
really thinks of us, and the thought of his presence produces
more fear than comfort in our hearts. It all gets to the very
heart of the message of the gospel.

Jesus lived the perfect life you and I never, ever could have
lived, and now his righteousness is credited to our account by
faith. He died the death that we should have died. His death
satisfied the Father's anger with our sin. He rose again, conquer-
ing sin and death so that we would know life eternal too. All
of this was done so that the chasm between us and God would
be bridged, so that we would be fully and eternally accepted
into his family, never again to face his rejection, never again to
pay the penalty for our sins, and free from having to measure

up to his standard in order to garner his love. What needed to be done, Jesus did. The work is complete.

Now, having said that, it is true that you have been called to work. You have been called to give yourself to the work of God's kingdom and to daily obey the commands of the King. You've been called to recognize that your life is no longer your own because you were bought with a price. But the work you do is never to be done in order to earn something. The work you're called to do is to be done in celebration of something. You don't work to earn God's favor; rather, your work is a hymn of thanks for the favor that Christ achieved on your behalf. You don't have to wonder if you've worked enough. You don't have to fear that you'll mess up and get booted out of the family. You don't have to fear seeing the back of God's head. You don't have to be haunted by the question of whether you've done enough for long enough. The bridge of impossibility has been walked by Christ. The job is done. Your relationship with God is eternally secure. Now, in thankfulness, go out and do his work in faith.

FOR FURTHER STUDY AND ENCOURAGEMENT
Luke 1:67–79

DAY 5

*Jesus paid it all! There are no bills due for your
sin! You are now free to simply trust and obey.*

STOP TRYING TO EARN SOMETHING from God. Stop trying to
gain more of his acceptance. Stop trying to earn his favor. Stop
trying to win his allegiance. Stop trying to do something that
would pay for his blessing. Stop trying to morally buy your
way out of his anger. Stop trying to reach a level where you
will know lasting peace with him. Just stop trying. Just stop.

So many Christians load onto their shoulders a burden that
they do not have to bear. They get up every morning and pick
up the heavy load of trying somehow, some way to achieve
something with God. They work hard to exercise what they
do not have in hopes they can achieve what is impossible. It
simply cannot work. So where does it lead? It leads either to
the scary pride of self-righteousness—a culture of moralistic
self-backslappers, who have no problem judging those who
have not achieved the level of righteousness they think that they
have—or to fear and discouragement—a culture of people who
don't run to God with their sin because they're afraid of him.

Paul wipes out this distorted, debilitating "buy your way
into grace" culture with a striking economy of words: "Now
it is evident that no one is justified before God by the law"
(Gal. 3:11). It is a statement that requires no preamble and
no amendment. No one is ever accepted by God because he
or she has kept the law. No one. That's it; no compromises

and no deals are needed. They are not needed because, first, it is impossible to buy your way into God's favor because sin makes you a lawbreaker and, second, your bills were fully and completely paid in the single payment of the cross of Jesus Christ. Christ did not make the first payment on your moral mortgage; he paid your entire moral mortgage in one single payment so that you could live in relationship to God debt-free forever. God's law is not your payment plan because there is no payment plan when the demands of a mortgage have been satisfied once and forever in one single payment.

So stop trying to measure up to get whatever from God. Stop hiding from him when you mess up. Stop comparing yourself to other people, wondering if God loves you less because you're not as "good" as them. Stop naming the good things you do as righteousness that not only gets you closer to God, but also proves to others that you are. Just stop asking the law to do what only grace can achieve, and start resting in the fact that you don't have any moral bills due because Jesus paid them all on the cross. And when you sin, don't pretend you didn't, don't panic, and don't hide. Run to Jesus in faith and receive mercy in your time of need, the kind of mercy he paid for you to have.

FOR FURTHER STUDY AND ENCOURAGEMENT
Isaiah 53

DAY 6

You were hardwired to depend on God, so your
dreams of self-reliance and self-sufficiency will
prove to be more nightmares than dreams.

WHY IS IT SO HARD for so many of us to ask for help? Why
is it so difficult for us to admit that we don't know things?
Why do we attempt to do things that we've never done before
without seeking instruction? Why is it so hard for us to admit
that we can't make it on our own? Why do we struggle to own
our weakness and our ignorance? Why do children resist the
instruction of their parents? Why do workers hate to be told
what to do by their bosses? Why do we not like to ask for direc-
tions? Why do we work so hard to present ourselves as more
ready, knowledgeable, and capable than we really are? Why do
we often push people away when they are offering assistance?
Why do we tell people that we're okay when we're not? Why
do we act as if we can solve things that we don't really understand? Why do we hesitate to get the advice of the doctor, the
counselor, or the wise friend? Why do we allow independence
to trouble our trouble? Why?

The answer seems too straightforward and simplistic, but
it is the answer nonetheless. The answer to every one of the
questions above is *sin*. Self-reliance and self-sufficiency are what
sin does to the heart. Hosea 10:13 captures this very powerfully: "You have plowed iniquity; you have reaped injustice;
you have eaten the fruit of lies. Because you have trusted in

amazon Gift Receipt

Send a Thank You Note

You can learn more about your gift or start a return here too.

Scan using the Amazon app or visit
https://a.co/66tqU84

40 Days of Faith
Order ID: 114-6431983-2293022 Ordered on June 20, 2021

your own way and in the multitude of your warriors." Don't miss the cause-and-effect structure of this passage. The prophet essentially asks: "Why have you experienced moral impurity? Why have you endured injustice? Why have you accepted what is not true?" There is only one possible answer to these questions, and it's not the one we want to hear. All of these things happened, the prophet says, because you wanted and trusted your own way and relied upon your own strength.

It is hard to accept, but vital to humbly admit. Bad things happen when we attempt to live as we were not created to live. Sin causes us to deny our need for God and others. Sin causes us to assign to ourselves the wisdom, strength, and righteousness we do not have. Sin causes us to dethrone God and enthrone ourselves. Sin is shockingly proud and self-assured. Sin really does cause us all to fall into the delusion that we can be like God. And because sin does this to all of us, it is dark, deceitful, and dangerous. Self-reliance and self-sufficiency as your fundamental approach to life will never lead to anything good. Sin always leads to death of some kind in some way. So we need to be rescued from our quest for independence and brought into a faith-based relationship with the one who really does have everything we need. And that's exactly what the grace of Jesus does for us!

FOR FURTHER STUDY AND ENCOURAGEMENT
James 3:13–16

DAY 7

True faith lives on the basis of two unshakable realities—that God really does exist and that he always rewards those who seek him.

Grace has positioned me
on two foundation stones
that have redefined
my identity,
redirected my purpose,
reshaped my desires,
rescued my thoughts,
and reformed my living.
I have new reason
to get up in the morning
and face my day
with courage,
hope,
joy,
confidence,
and rest.

Your grace has changed
everything,
for it has made me
sure
that you exist
and that
you reward
those who seek you (Heb. 11:6).

FOR FURTHER STUDY AND ENCOURAGEMENT
Hebrews 11:1–22

DAY 8

If your heart isn't ruled by God's honor and
your life by God's plan, you may seem religious,
but what you're living isn't biblical faith.

I WANT TO USE MARRIAGE as a case study for the principle stated above. None of us has lived in a marriage that is completely free of conflict and tension. None of us has been able to escape moments of irritation and impatience. We all have had nasty arguments or extended moments of silence. We all have been disappointed in our marriages in some way. (If you're single, apply everything I've said to the relationships in your life.) Now, you just have to ask, "What is all that tension and conflict about?" If you were to read the average Christian marriage book, you would be led to conclude that all of the fights and quarrels are about the inescapable horizontal issues within every marriage. So the conclusion is that if you are smart enough to discuss gender differences, personality differences, role expectations, finances, sex, parenting, diet, and so on, you will be able to avoid most of those conflicts.

On the surface, it sounds right, but it isn't what the Bible says. Consider the following provocative passage:

> What causes quarrels and what causes fights among you?
> Is it not this, that your passions are at war within you? You
> desire and do not have, so you murder. You covet and cannot
> obtain, so you fight and quarrel. You do not have, because
> you do not ask. You ask and do not receive, because you ask
> wrongly, to spend it on your passions. You adulterous people!

22

Do you not know that friendship with the world is enmity with God? Therefore whoever wishes to be a friend of the world makes himself an enemy of God. Or do you suppose it is to no purpose that the Scripture says, "He yearns jealously over the spirit that he has made to dwell in us"? But he gives more grace. Therefore it says, "God opposes the proud, but gives grace to the humble." Submit yourselves therefore to God. Resist the devil, and he will flee from you. Draw near to God, and he will draw near to you. Cleanse your hands, you sinners, and purify your hearts, you double-minded. Be wretched and mourn and weep. Let your laughter be turned to mourning and your joy to gloom. Humble yourselves before the Lord, and he will exalt you. (James 4:1–10)

Notice how James explains why we have so many fights and quarrels. He doesn't say, "They come from those difficult people you live with" or "They are the result of the practical issues that you're forced to deal with." No, he says they come from the "passions" that wage war in our hearts. In this context, *passion* means a powerful, ruling desire. I fight with you because I have a heart problem. Rather than my heart being ruled by God and motivated by God's honor, my heart is ruled by my wants, my needs, and my feelings. If it is, I am always in some kind of conflict with you. Furthermore, James tells us that human conflict is rooted in spiritual adultery. When we put ourselves where God alone belongs, conflict always results. It is all just another argument for the essentiality of God's grace in Jesus.

FOR FURTHER STUDY AND ENCOURAGEMENT
Isaiah 29 (especially v. 13)

DAY 9

*There is a significant difference between
amazement and faith. God doesn't just want to
blow your mind; he wants to rule your heart.*

IT IS AN IMPORTANT DISTINCTION, one that is not made frequently enough. Faith surely does engage your brain, but it is fundamentally more than that. Faith is something that you do with your life. True biblical faith doesn't stop with thought; it radically rearranges the way that you approach everything in your life. Amazement is what you experience when you are taken beyond the categories that you carry around to explain or define things. Amazement is a step in the faith process, but there is a huge difference between amazement and faith.

Pretend you're standing next to me on a pier on the Jersey Shore. We're looking at one of those amusement park contraptions that is essentially a fifty-foot-high slingshot, into which they strap some otherwise sane human being and launch him back and forth over the Atlantic Ocean in the night. Now, that ride amazes both of us, but we're not about to strap in and let ourselves be launched into the night. Amazed? Yes, but we will not put our faith in that thing. In the same way:

- You can be amazed by the grand sweep of the redemptive story in Scripture and not be living by faith.
- You can be amazed by the labyrinthine logic of the theology of the word of God and not be living by faith.

- You can be amazed by the great worship music you participate in every Sunday and not be living by faith.
- You can be amazed by the love of your small group and not be living by faith.
- You can be amazed by the wonderful biblical preaching and teaching that you hear and not be living by faith.
- You can be amazed by the grace of the cross of Jesus and not be living by faith.

There is a significant, yes, even profound difference between amazement and faith. God will not leave us in a state of amazement. He works by grace to craft us into people of settled, hopeful, courageous, active, celebratory, God-glorifying faith. He will settle for nothing less. He is not satisfied with the wonder of our minds. He will not relent until he has established his life-altering rule in our hearts. He works so that we really will "believe that he exists and that he rewards those who seek him" (Heb. 11:6). You can't work that faith up in yourself. It is a gift of his grace. The cross makes that gift available to you right here, right now.

FOR FURTHER STUDY AND ENCOURAGEMENT
John 20:24–29

DAY 10

*It never works to ask people to do for you what
only God can do. It never works to wait for God
to do what he has clearly called you to do.*

HERE'S THE PRINCIPLE (which surely is easier to write out than
it is to live): you can't look horizontally for what you will get
only vertically, and you can't wait vertically for what you have
been called to do horizontally. We all get these two confused
again and again. Many a wife believes it is her husband's duty
to bring her happiness. Such a woman is actually acting as if
it's okay to put her inner sense of well-being in the hands of
another human being. The person next to you is never a safe
source of your happiness because that person is flawed and
will inevitably fail you in some way. Only God is ever a safe
keeper of the security, peace, and rest of your soul. Here is the
bottom line—earth will never be your savior. Earth was created
to point you to the one who alone is able to give peace and
rest to your searching heart. Yet today many people, who say
they believe in God, shop horizontally for what can be found
only vertically.

On the other hand, there are many people who give in to
the temptation to do the opposite. They wait for God to do
for them what he has clearly called and empowered them to
do. I've heard many people who were dealing with fractured
relationships say to me, "I'm just waiting for the Lord to rec-
oncile our relationship." It sounds spiritual, but it is simply

26

wrong. If you have something against your brother, if there is conflict between you, the Bible tells you to get up, go, and be reconciled to him. When it came time for Israel to enter the promised land, God was going to part the waters of the Jordan River, but he commanded the priests to step into it. God was going to defeat Jericho, but he called his children to walk around it. God promises to provide, but he calls us to labor, pray, and give. God alone has the power to save, but he calls us to witness, testify, proclaim, teach, live, and preach. You see, God not only determines outcomes, but he rules over the means by which those outcomes are realized.

So the life of faith is all about rest and work. We rest in God's presence and constant care (vertical), and we toil with our hands, busy at the work that we have been commanded to do (horizontal). We rest in our work and work in our rest. At times, we work because we believe that God who is at work calls us to work. At others times, we rest from our work because we believe that the work that needs to be done only God can do. So rest and work, and work and rest. It is the rhythm of the life of faith.

FOR FURTHER STUDY AND ENCOURAGEMENT

Matthew 19:16–30

DAY 11

*Faith means you take God at his word, you
never let yourself think that you're smarter than
him, and you live inside his boundaries.*

FAITH SO COMPLETELY TAKES GOD at his word that it is willing
to do what he says and stay inside his boundaries. Faith is a
response of your heart to God that completely alters the way
you live your life. You don't just think by faith; you live by faith.

Now, it is important to face two implications of real, living
faith. First, faith is simply never natural for us. We aren't born
with faith in God. We don't come out of the womb ready to
acknowledge his existence, worship him for his glory, and
submit to his rules. We tend to live by sight, by personal experience, by collective research, or by good old intuition, but
faith isn't natural. It's natural to give yourself to wonderment
about mysteries in your life you'll never solve. It's natural to
imagine where you'll be in ten or twenty years. It's natural to
wonder why someone else's life has turned out so very differ-
ently from yours. It's natural to panic at moments, wondering
if God really does exist and, if he does, if he hears your prayers.
But putting your entire existence in the hands of one whom
you cannot see, touch, or hear is far from natural. This is why
faith is only ever a gift of divine grace. You and I have all the
power in the world to doubt and no independent power at
all to believe. So if you are living by faith, don't proudly pat
yourself on the back as if you did something great. No, raise

28

your eyes and your hands toward heaven and thank God for gifting you with the desire and ability to believe.

Second, participating in formal Christianity is a part of a life of faith, but it does not define the life of faith. Just because you participate in the scheduled programs of your church doesn't mean you're a person of faith. You can praise God for his wisdom in that service on Sunday but be breaking his law on Tuesday because, at street level, you really do think you're smarter than him. You can sing in thanks for his grace on Sunday and resist the work of that grace the rest of the week. It's so easy to swindle yourself into believing that you're living by faith when you're really not. So look into the mirror of Hebrews 11 and examine your faith. You don't need to do that fearfully, anxious at what you'll see. You don't need to deny the reality of your spiritual struggle or act as if you're something that you're not. You don't have to fear exposure, because your struggle of faith has been more than adequately addressed by the grace of the cross of the Lord Jesus. Run to him and confess the off-and-on-again faith of your heart. He will not turn you away.

FOR FURTHER STUDY AND ENCOURAGEMENT
Luke 7:1–17

DAY 12

Today you'll wonder if you'll have enough, or you'll tell yourself, "The Lord will provide," and in faith you'll move forward.

TO LIVE THE WAY YOU HAVE been called and graced to live, you have to know your address. You have to understand what it means to live where you live every day. For example, if you live in the city, you know that parking is going to be a problem. If you live in the suburbs, you know you'll have a big yard that will require maintenance. If you live in the inner city, you may need to be aware of the dangers on the streets at night. If you live in an old house, you can be sure that you'll need to hone your carpentry, electricity, and plumbing skills, because some parts of the structure are going to give way. The same is true spiritually. It is essential that you understand the implications of living where you live or you'll find yourself confused and unprepared over and over again.

You and I live between the "already" and the "not yet." Jesus has made the ultimate sacrifice. The wisdom of the word has been placed in your hands. The Holy Spirit has come to live inside you. But the work of God in you, for you, and through you has not yet been completed. This means that sin has not yet been fully eradicated and you are not yet all that grace will transform you to be. The last enemy of God has not yet been placed under the powerful foot of the Messiah. So the moral battle still rages. The spiritual war still goes on. That means you need to understand that you live in a war zone. And you need to be very clear on this—that great spiritual war is fought on the turf of your heart and it's fought for control of your soul. Your life is lived every day in the middle of that war. It's a war of doubt and faith. It's a war of submission and rebellion. It's a war of anxiety and trust. It's a war of wisdom and foolishness. It's a war of hope and despair. It's a war of allegiance and disloyalty. It's a war.

Perhaps the epicenter of that war is this question: "Will the Lord do what he has promised?" Will the Lord provide? Can I step out in faith and courage, knowing that the Lord is with me and will provide what I need when I need it? Or do I have to worry that, when it comes to push and shove, I won't have enough? Should I be afraid, or is God trustworthy?

When you hit hard times, when your weakness is exposed, be ready for the enemy to whisper in your ear, "Where is your God now?" and be ready to respond, "He is where he has been and always will be—with me in power, glory, and grace." You won't always feel his nearness, but you can rest assured he will never abandon you. He is the one who said, "Behold, I am with you always" (Matt. 28:20), and he never goes back on his word.

FOR FURTHER STUDY AND ENCOURAGEMENT
Psalm 22

DAY 13

God calls you to persevere by faith, and then, with
powerful grace, he protects and keeps you.

IT IS A WONDERFULLY ENCOURAGING name for the God you serve, yet it's possible to let it pass through your eyes and into your brain without stopping to celebrate its glory. In Romans 15:5, Paul calls your Lord "the God of endurance." This title really gets at the center of where your hope is to be found. Let me state it plainly: your hope is not to be found in your willingness and ability to endure, but in God's unshakable, enduring commitment to never turn from his work of grace. Your hope is that you have been welcomed into communion with one who will endure no matter what.

Why is this so important to understand? Because your endurance will be spotty at best. There will be moments when you will forget who you are and live as a grace amnesiac. There will be times when you will get discouraged and for a while quit doing the good things God calls you to do. There will be moments, big and small, when you will willingly rebel. You may be thinking, "Not me." But think with me—when you, as a Christian, say something nasty to another person, you don't do it because you're ignorant that it is wrong, but because at that point you don't give a rip about what is wrong.

You see, perfect endurance demands just that, perfection, and since none of us is there yet, we must look outside ourselves for hope. Your hope of enduring is not to be found in your character or strength, but in your Lord's. Because he will ever be faithful, you can bank on the fact that he will give you what you need to be faithful too. Your perseverance rests on him, and he defines what endurance looks like! It is the grace of endurance granted to you by the God of endurance that provides you with everything you need to continue to be what he calls you to be and do what he calls you to do between this moment and the moment when you cross over to the other side. When difficulty exposes the weakness of your resolve and the limits of your strength, you do not have to panic, because he will endure even in those moments when you don't feel able to do so yourself.

FOR FURTHER STUDY AND ENCOURAGEMENT
1 Timothy 6:11–16

DAY 14

*Faith isn't natural for us. Doubt is, fear is,
and pride is, but faith in the words and works
of another isn't, and for that there's grace.*

GOD HASN'T JUST FORGIVEN YOU—praise him that he has—but he has also called you to a brand-new way of living. He has called you to live by faith. Now, here's the rub. Faith is not normal for us. Faith is frankly a counterintuitive way for us to live. Doubt is quite natural for us. Wondering what God is doing is natural. It's normal to think your life is harder than that of others. Envying the life of someone else is natural. Wishing life were easier and that you had more control is natural. It's typical for you and me to try to figure out the future. Worry is natural. Fear is natural. Wanting to give up is natural. It's natural to wonder if all of your good habits make a difference in the end. It's normal to be occasionally haunted by the question of whether what you have staked your life on is really true. But faith isn't natural.

This means that faith isn't something you can work up inside yourself. As we saw earlier, faith comes to you as God's gift of grace: "For by grace you have been saved through faith. And this is not your own doing; it is the gift of God" (Eph. 2:8). Not only is your salvation a gift of God, but the faith to embrace it is his gift as well. But here is what you need to understand: God not only gives you the grace to believe for your salvation, but he also works to enable you to live by faith. If you are living by faith, you know that you have been visited by powerful transforming grace, because that way of living just isn't normal for you and me. If your way of living is no longer based on what your eyes can see and your mind can understand, but on God's presence, promises, principles, and provisions, it is because God has crafted faith in you.

Could it be that all of those things that come your way that confuse you and that you never would've chosen for yourself are God's tools to build your faith? By progressive transforming grace, he is enabling you to live the brand-new life he calls all of his children to live—the Godward life for which you were created. You don't have to hide in guilt when weak faith gets you off the path, because your hope in life isn't your faithfulness but his. You can run in weakness and once again seek his strength. And you can know that in zealous grace he will not leave his craftwork until faith fully rules your heart unchallenged. He always gives freely what we need in order to do what he has called us to do.

FOR FURTHER STUDY AND ENCOURAGEMENT
Hebrews 11:23–40

DAY 15

*Faith is about measuring your potential, not on
the basis of your natural gifts and experience, but
in the surety of God's presence and promises.*

IT IS ALMOST A HUMOROUS STORY. It's found in Judges 6:11–18:

Now the angel of the LORD came and sat under the terebinth
at Ophrah, which belonged to Joash the Abiezrite, while his
son Gideon was beating out wheat in the winepress to hide
it from the Midianites. And the angel of the LORD appeared
to him and said to him, "The LORD is with you, O mighty
man of valor." And Gideon said to him, "Please, sir, if the
LORD is with us, why then has all this happened to us? And
where are all his wonderful deeds that our fathers recounted
to us, saying, 'Did not the LORD bring us up from Egypt?'
But now the LORD has forsaken us and given us into the
hand of Midian." And the LORD turned to him and said,
"Go in this might of yours and save Israel from the hand of
Midian; do not I send you?" And he said to him, "Please,
Lord, how can I save Israel? Behold, my clan is the weakest
in Manasseh, and I am the least in my father's house." And
the LORD said to him, "But I will be with you, and you shall
strike the Midianites as one man." And he said to him, "If
now I have found favor in your eyes, then show me a sign
that it is you who speak with me. Please do not depart from
here until I come to you and bring out my present and set it
before you." And he said, "I will stay till you return."

God approaches Gideon to call him to lead Israel in a very important battle and calls him a "mighty man of valor." Where does he find this "mighty man"? He finds him threshing wheat in a winepress. He's doing something indoors that you normally do outdoors because he is afraid of the very people whom God is going to call him to attack! God calls him a mighty man not because of Gideon's natural strength and courage, but because of what Gideon will be able to do in the power that God will give him. We know this is true because God begins his statement with these words: "The LORD is with you." Poor fearful Gideon even questions that.

Then Gideon essentially says: "God, you must have the wrong address. I'm the least son of the most inconsequential tribe in all of Israel. How in the world do you expect me to save Israel?" As this statement reveals, Gideon both misunderstands who he is and who God is. If you fail to remember who God is in his power, glory, and grace, and you forget who you are as a child in his family, you will always mismeasure your potential to do what God has called you to do. You will measure your capability based on your natural gifts and the size of whatever it is that God has chosen you to face. Thankfully, since God is with you, you have been blessed with wisdom and power beyond your own that give you potential you would not have on your own.

FOR FURTHER STUDY AND ENCOURAGEMENT
1 Corinthians 1:26–31

DAY 16

*Real faith never calls you to swindle yourself into
thinking that things are better than they are.
Biblical faith is shockingly honest and hopeful.*

BIBLICAL FAITH IS NOT ABOUT wearing a saccharine smile while living in a constant state of religious denial. It's not about covering the stark and dark realities of a fallen world with overused pseudobiblical clichés. It's not about praying in King James English because somehow that makes you feel more spiritual. It's not about priding yourself on your ability to keep God's rules or thinking you're more sanctified because you're on pace to read through the whole Bible again this year. It's not about cleaning yourself up on Sunday so your public persona hides the real details of your private spiritual life. It's not about keeping score of how many years you've gone through without missing a worship service. It's not about polishing your righteousness so you look better to yourself and to others. It's not about saying you're okay when you give daily empirical evidence that you are anything but okay. If you are doing, saying, or thinking religious things that are meant to protect you from reality, you are not living biblical Christianity. You may feel better, but your heart has not been quieted by biblical faith. The faith of the Bible will never call you to deny reality in any way. The faith of the Bible is so in awe of the grandeur and glory of God that it is able to look at the darkest of realities in life and not be afraid.

Abraham did not need to deny reality in order to leave his home without knowing for sure where God was taking him. Noah did not need to deny reality in order to spend 120 years building that ark. The children of Israel did not need to deny reality in order to walk around Jericho for seven days. David did not need to deny reality in order to face Goliath in battle. Shadrach, Meshach, and Abednego did not need to deny reality in order to step into that white-hot furnace. Peter didn't need to deny reality in order to stand before the Sanhedrin and refuse to quit preaching the gospel. You see, it wasn't the naïveté of faith that propelled these people. No, it was the clarity of faith that caused them to do what they did.

It is only when you look at this dark world through the lens of the existence, power, authority, wisdom, faithfulness, love, and grace of the King of kings and Lord of lords that you see reality with clarity. You cannot ever assess and understand what you are facing if you omit the fact of facts—the existence of God. In fact, as we have seen, that's how the writer of Hebrews defines faith: "And without faith it is impossible to please him, for whoever would draw near to God must *believe that he exists* and that he rewards those who seek him" (11:6).

Are you lacking faith? Run to the one who freely gives it as his gift of grace to you.

FOR FURTHER STUDY AND ENCOURAGEMENT
Daniel 3:8–30

DAY 17

God calls you to grow in your faith and
then feeds you with the growth-producing
nutrients of his grace and truth.

ARE YOU GROWING IN YOUR FAITH? Do you care if you're not? Have you become satisfied with a little bit of Bible knowledge and a little bit of doctrinal understanding? Have you stopped feeding on the spiritual food of God's grace even though that grace has not yet come anywhere near to finishing its work in you? Do you hunger for the grace you've been given to continue to do its transforming work in the places where there's evidence that there's more work to be done? Are you satisfied with being a little more religious or a little more spiritual? Could it be that you claim to be a believer, but are satisfied to have parts of your life shaped by other values? Does your relationship with God really shape the way you think about and act in your marriage, in your friendships, in your parenting, in your job, in your finances, as a citizen or neighbor, in your private pursuits, or in your secret thoughts and desires? As you examine yourself, are you able to be satisfied in places where God is not? Are you pursuing the grace that you've been given because you know that you regularly demonstrate that you are not yet a grace graduate?

When I think on this topic, my mind immediately runs to two passages:

So put away all malice and all deceit and hypocrisy and envy and all slander. Like newborn infants, long for the pure

spiritual milk, that by it you may grow up into salvation—
if indeed you have tasted that the Lord is good.

As you come to him, a living stone rejected by men but
in the sight of God chosen and precious, you yourselves like
living stones are being built up as a spiritual house, to be
a holy priesthood, to offer spiritual sacrifices acceptable to
God through Jesus Christ. (1 Pet. 2:1–5)

About this we have much to say, and it is hard to explain,
since you have become dull of hearing. For though by this
time you ought to be teachers, you need someone to teach
you again the basic principles of the oracles of God. You
need milk, not solid food, for everyone who lives on milk is
unskilled in the word of righteousness, since he is a child. But
solid food is for the mature, for those who have their powers
of discernment trained by constant practice to distinguish
good from evil. (Heb. 5:11–14)

Be honest today—which passage best describes you? Are you
that ravenous baby who can't get enough of his mother's milk or
the person who should be mature enough to digest solid food,
but isn't ready? Remember, you don't have to defend yourself or
deny the evidence—the grace of Jesus has freed you from that.
The cross of Jesus welcomes you to be honest because all the
places where you need to be honest have been covered by the
blood of Jesus. And remember too that it takes grace to admit
how much you still need grace. That grace is yours in Jesus.

FOR FURTHER STUDY AND ENCOURAGEMENT
Hebrews 5:11–6:12

DAY 18

*When hardship comes your way, will you tell yourself
it's a tool of God's grace and a sign of his love,
or will you give in to doubting his goodness?*

IF YOU ARE NOT ON GOD'S redemptive agenda page, you will
end up doubting his goodness. One of the most important
questions you could ask is: "What is God doing in the here
and now?" The follow-up question is also important: "How
should I respond to it?" It is nearly impossible to think about
life properly and to live appropriately if you are fundamentally
confused about what God is doing. If someone were to ask
you the first of those two questions, how would you respond?
Are you tracking with God's agenda? Are you after what God's
after? Are you living in a way that is consistent with what
God is doing? Do you struggle with questions of God's love,
faithfulness, wisdom, and goodness? Do you ever envy the life
of another? Do you sometimes feel alone? Do you fall into
thinking that no one understands what you're going through?
Are you ever plagued by doubts as to whether Christianity is
true after all? If you aren't struggling with these things, are you
near someone who is?

Here's the bottom line. Right here, right now, God isn't
so much working to deliver to you your personal definition
of happiness. He's not committed to give you a predictable
schedule, happy relationships, or comfortable surroundings.
He hasn't promised you a successful career, a nice place to live,

42

and a community of people who appreciate you. What he has promised you is *himself*, and what he brings to you is the zeal of his transforming grace. No, he's not first working on your happiness; he's committed to your holiness. That doesn't mean he is offering you less than you've hoped for, but much, much more. In grace, he is intent on delivering you from your greatest, deepest, and most long-term problem: sin. He offers you gifts of grace that transcend the moment, that literally are of eternal value. He has not unleashed his power in your life only to deliver to you things that quickly pass away and that have no capacity at all to satisfy your heart.

This means that often when you are tempted to think that God is loving you less because your life is hard, he is actually loving you more. The hardships that you are facing are the tool of his exposing, forgiving, liberating, and transforming grace. These hard moments aren't in your life because God is distant and uncaring, but rather because he loves you so fully. These moments become moments of faith and not doubt when by grace you begin to value what God says is truly valuable. Do you value what God values?

FOR FURTHER STUDY AND ENCOURAGEMENT

James 1:12–18

DAY 19

*Sure, you'll face difficulty. God is prying open
your fingers so you'll let go of your dreams,
rest in his comforts, and take up his call.*

THINK ABOUT THE WORDS PENNED by Peter near the beginning of his New Testament letter: "Now for a little while, if necessary, you have been grieved by various trials, so that the tested genuineness of your faith—more precious than gold that perishes though it is tested by fire—may be found to result in praise and glory and honor at the revelation of Jesus Christ" (1 Pet. 1:6–7).

As he opens his letter, Peter gives us a past-present-future summary of God's redemptive plan, but his interest is really in what God is doing right here, right now between Christ's first and second comings. Of all of the words that he could use to describe what God is doing now, he selects these three: *grieved, trials,* and *tested.* These are three words that most of us hope will never describe our lives. None of us gets up in the morning and prays, "Lord, if you love me, you will send more suffering my way today." Rather, when we are living in the middle of difficulty, we are tempted to view it as a sign of God's unfaithfulness or inattention.

Peter, however, doesn't see moments of difficulty as obstacles in the way of God's plan or indications that his plan has failed. No, for him they are an important part of God's plan. Rather than being signs of his inattention, they are sure signs of the zeal of his redemptive love. In grace, he leads you where you didn't plan to go in order to produce in you what you couldn't achieve on your own. In these moments, he works to alter the values of your heart so that you let go of your little kingdom of one and give yourself to his kingdom of glory and grace.

God is working right now, but not so much to give us predictable, comfortable, and pleasurable lives. He isn't so much working to transform our circumstances as he is working through hard circumstances to transform you and me. Perhaps in hard moments, when we are tempted to wonder where God's grace is, it is grace that we are getting, but not grace in the form of a soft pillow or a cool drink. Rather, in those moments, we are being blessed with the heart-transforming grace of difficulty because the God who loves us knows that this is exactly the grace we need.

FOR FURTHER STUDY AND ENCOURAGEMENT
James 1:2–11

DAY 20

*The difficulties of your life are not in the way
of God's plan; they are a tool of it. They're
crafted to advance his work of grace.*

PERHAPS THE TWO MOST IMPORTANT questions you could ask between your conversion and your final resurrection are:

1. What in the world is God doing right here, right now?
2. How in the world should I respond to what God is doing?

The way that you answer these questions determines, in a real way, the character of your faith and the direction of your life. Consider how James answers these questions in the very first part of his letter:

Count it all joy, my brothers, when you meet trials of various kinds, for you know that the testing of your faith produces steadfastness. And let steadfastness have its full effect, that you may be perfect and complete, lacking in nothing.

If any of you lacks wisdom, let him ask God, who gives generously to all without reproach, and it will be given him. But let him ask in faith, with no doubting, for the one who doubts is like a wave of the sea that is driven and tossed by the wind. For that person must not suppose that he will receive anything from the Lord; he is a double-minded man, unstable in all his ways.

Let the lowly brother boast in his exaltation, and the rich in his humiliation, because like a flower of the grass he

46

will pass away. For the sun rises with its scorching heat and withers the grass; its flower falls, and its beauty perishes. So also will the rich man fade away in the midst of his pursuits.

Blessed is the man who remains steadfast under trial, for when he has stood the test he will receive the crown of life, which God has promised to those who love him. (1:2–12)

What is God doing in the here and now? He is employing the difficulties of life as tools of grace to produce character in you that would not grow any other way. So your trials are not a sign that God has forgotten you or is being unfaithful to his promises. Rather, they stand as a reminder that he is committed to his grace and will not forsake it—it *will* complete its work. No, he's not exercising his power to make your life easy. No, he's not at work trying to deliver your particular definition of happiness. He's giving you much more than that—eternally faithful, forgiving, and transforming grace.

And what should your response be? James says, "remain steadfast under trial." Don't become discouraged and give up. Don't listen to the lies of the enemy. Don't forsake your good habits of faith. Don't question God's goodness. Look at your trials and see grace. Behind those difficulties is an ever-present Redeemer who is completing his work.

FOR FURTHER STUDY AND ENCOURAGEMENT

Hebrews 12:3–11

DAY 21

The best theology will not remove mystery from
your life, so rest is found in trusting the one
who rules, is all, and knows no mystery.

HER VOICE QUIVERED THAT MORNING as she told me to get home as quickly as I could. My wife, Luella, is a very emotionally stable woman. She isn't easily rocked. I knew what we were facing was serious because it *had* rocked her. I was about six hours away; with my assistant, I made the nervous trip home.

Nicole, our daughter, had started her walk home from work late the previous night, as she had done many nights before. A car driven by a drunk and unlicensed driver careered up on the sidewalk and crushed Nicole against a wall. She had devastating injuries, including eleven breaks of her pelvis and massive internal bleeding. When I finally got to the hospital and walked into Nicole's intensive-care room, I did what any father with a drop of parental blood in him would do. I fell apart. I crawled up on Nicole's bed, not sure if she could hear me, and said, "It's Dad, you're not alone, and God is with you, too."

When I walked into that room, it was as if the whole world went dark. My heart cried, "Why, why, why?" If I could choose, I wouldn't have any of my children go through such a thing. And if I had had to choose one of my children, I wouldn't have chosen Nicole at that moment in her life; she seemed so vulnerable. In an instant, we were cast into life-changing mystery, and our theological non-negotiables didn't take that mystery away. Nicole did recover well, but we lived through four years of travail.

I held onto the thought that our lives were not out of control. We were comforted again and again with the thought that when it came to Nicole's accident, God was neither surprised nor afraid. You see, there is no mystery with God. He is never caught off guard. He never wonders how he is going to deal with the unexpected thing. I love the words of Daniel 2:22: "He knows what is in the darkness, and light dwells with him."

God is with you in your moments of darkness because he will never leave you. But your darkness isn't dark to him. Your mysteries aren't mysterious to him. Your surprises don't surprise him. He understands all the things that confuse you the most. Not only are your mysteries not mysterious to him, but he is in complete charge of all that is mysterious to you and me.

Remember today that there is one who looks at what you see as dark and sees light. And as you remember that, remember, too, that he is the ultimate definition of everything that is wise, good, true, loving, and faithful. He holds both you and your mysteries in his gracious hands, and because he does, you can find rest even when the darkness of mystery has entered your door.

FOR FURTHER STUDY AND ENCOURAGEMENT
Isaiah 40:12–31

DAY 22

*Don't be discouraged today. You can leave your
"what-ifs" and "if-onlys" in the hands of the
one who loves you and rules all things.*

EVEN THOUGH YOU'RE A PERSON of faith who has acquired some degree of biblical literacy and theological knowledge, there's one thing you can be sure of—God will confuse you. Your theology will give you only a limited ability to exegete your experiences. The commands, principles, and case studies of Scripture will take you only so far in your quest to figure out your life. There will be moments when you simply don't understand what is going on. In fact, you will face moments when what God, who has declared himself to be good, brings into your life won't seem good. It may even seem bad, very bad.

Now, if your faith is based on your ability to fully understand your past, present, and future, then your moments of confusion will become moments of weakening faith. But the reality is that you are not left with only two options—understand everything and rest in peace or understand little and be tormented by anxiety. There is a third way. It really is the way of true biblical faith. The Bible tells you that real peace is found in resting in the wisdom of the one who holds all of your "what-ifs" and "if-onlys" in his loving hands. Isaiah captures this well with these comforting words: "You keep him in perfect peace whose mind is stayed on you, because he trusts in you" (Isa. 26:3).

Real, sturdy, lasting peace, peace that doesn't rise and fall with circumstances, isn't to be found in picking apart your life until you have understood all of the components. You will never understand it all because God, for your good and his glory, keeps some of it shrouded in mystery. So peace is found only in trust, trust of the one who is in careful control of all the things that tend to rob you of your peace. He knows, he understands, he is in control of what appears to be chaos, he is never surprised, he is never confused, he never worries or loses a night's sleep, he never walks off the job to take a rest, he never gets so busy with one thing that he neglects another, and he never plays favorites.

You need to remind yourself again and again of his wise and loving control, not because that will immediately make your life make sense, but because it will give you rest and peace in those moments that all of us face at one time or another—when life doesn't seem to make any sense.

FOR FURTHER STUDY AND ENCOURAGEMENT
Luke 12:22–34

DAY 23

*You can't hear him, but he's wiser; you can't see
him, but he's more faithful; you can't touch him,
but he's nearer than whatever else you'd trust.*

IT IS ONE OF THE MOST amazing statements of what only grace
can do. On the surface, it doesn't make any sense. If it were
not rooted in the most important fact of the universe that you
could ever consider, you would call the people involved "crazy."
It marks the fundamental dividing line of all human beings.
The apostle Peter is talking about believers living between the
"already" and the "not yet" when he says of their relationship
to Jesus Christ: "Though you have not seen him, you love
him. Though you do not now see him, you believe in him
and rejoice with joy that is inexpressible and filled with glory,
obtaining the outcome of your faith, the salvation of your
souls" (1 Pet. 1:8–9).

Now, allow yourself to consider the radical nature of what
this passage says about the deepest motivations of the hearts
of God's people. They have connected their deepest love, belief, joy, and faith to someone they have never seen, heard,
or touched. They have staked the hopes and dreams of their
lives to this invisible one. Their relationship to him is one of
life-altering love. When they think of him, they experience joy,
joy so deep that it cannot be expressed.

If it were not for the fact that the ultimate fact of human existence—the fact that gives meaning to every other fact—is the

existence, character, and plan of God, none of this would make any sense at all. You would stand back, look at these "believers," and conclude that they were delusional, crazy. But they are not crazy. They are the blessed ones, the enlightened ones, the ones whose hearts have been opened to the most important thing that your heart could embrace.

This is what grace does. It rescues us from our spiritual blindness. It releases us from our bondage to our rationalism and materialism. Grace gives us the faith to be utterly assured of what we cannot see. It frees us from refusing to believe in anything we cannot experience with our physical senses. But grace does more. It connects us to the invisible one in an eternal love relationship that fills us with joy we have never known before and gives us rest of heart that we would have thought impossible.

And that grace is still rescuing us, because we still tend to forget what is important, real, and true. We still tend to look to the physical world for our comfort. We still fail to remember in given moments that we really do have a heavenly Father. Grace has done a wonderful thing for us and continues to do more and more.

FOR FURTHER STUDY AND ENCOURAGEMENT
1 Peter 1:1–12

DAY 24

*If you trust only when you understand, you'll
live with lots of doubt. God's wisdom is bigger
than anything your mind can conceive.*

IT'S HUMBLING TO ADMIT, but important nonetheless. You will
never reach true, sturdy, and lasting peace and rest of heart by
means of understanding. "Why not?" you may ask. Because
there will always be things in your life that you do not understand. God reveals in his word all the things that you need
to know, but he does not tell you all the things that could be
known. He reveals his plan for all his people in his word, but
he does not tell you his individualized sovereign plan for you.
You and I simply are not able to contain in our limited brains
all of God's plans for us and all of the reasons for those plans.

Now, here's the rub: God created you to be a rational human
being. He designed you to think, that is, to strive to make
sense out of your life and your world. That is not a bad thing
in itself. In fact, it is a very good thing. Your ability to think,
interpret, examine, define, explain, and understand is meant
to drive you to God. Your mentality is meant to lead you to
him and to enable you to understand his revelation to you. So
biblical faith is not irrational, but you must face this: it will
take you beyond your ability to reason. You and I never could
have started at the fall of Adam and Eve and used reason to
predict the coming of Jesus and his death on the cross. Old
Testament believers knew that God was going to deal with sin

and give new life to his people because God told them that this was what he was going to do. But they did not know that the death of the Son of God would be the means by which this would happen.

In the same way, as we stand between the "already" and the "not yet," we can be assured of all that God has told us in his word, but we can also be sure that there is much that he has not told us about what is to come, personally and collectively. So there will be mysteries and surprises in our lives. If you and I suspend belief at every encounter with mystery, we will spend large portions of our lives not believing. If we question God's goodness and love every time he acts in a way that is unexpected, we will end up concluding that he is not good. If we refuse to rest when we don't understand, we will end up living lives of distress.

So where is peace and rest of heart to be found? You rest in the fact that in his word God has told you all the things you absolutely need to know, and then you rest in the complete perfection of his wisdom and character. You rest not because you know, but because the one who knows it all is the definition of what is wise and what is good.

FOR FURTHER STUDY AND ENCOURAGEMENT
1 Corinthians 1:18–25

DAY 25

If you put too many things in your need category,
you will end up frustrated with life, hurt by
others, and doubting God's goodness.

IT REALLY IS ONE OF the sloppiest words used in human culture. If *need* means "essential for life," then the vast majority of the things we say that we need we don't actually need. You know this if you have children or are around children. Let's say you're a parent and you have taken your child to the mall (which is your first mistake). As you're walking through the mall, your child sees the sneaker store and immediately makes a left-hand turn. Now, with nose pressed against the window of the store, he says, "Mom, I neeeeeeeed those sneakers." You look down at his feet, which are encased in perfectly good shoes, and you say: "No, I'm not getting you those sneakers. You already have perfectly good shoes." Now, when you say this, your child does not think: "What a wise mother I have been blessed with. She has seen through my distorted sense of need, has recognized selfish desire, and has lovingly rescued me from me." No, your child lashes out against you: "You always say 'no' to me. I don't know why I have to have the one mom who hates sneakers." Then your child refuses to relate to you for the rest of the time that you are in the mall.

When you tell yourself that something is a need, three things follow. First, you feel entitled to the thing, because, after all, it is a need. Second, because it is a need, you feel it's your right to demand it. And third, you then judge the love of another person by his or her willingness to deliver the thing. This not only happens in our relationships with one another, but more important, it happens in our relationship with God. When you name something as a need and God doesn't deliver it, you begin to doubt his goodness. What is deadly about this is that you simply don't run for help to someone whose character you've come to doubt.

In Matthew 6:32, Jesus reminds us that we have a heavenly Father who knows exactly what we need. There is confrontation and comfort in Jesus's words. The confrontation is this: the reason Jesus reminds us that we have a Father who has a clear understanding of our true needs is because we don't have such an understanding. We constantly get needs and wants confused, and when we do, we are tempted to question the love of our heavenly Father. The comfort is that, by grace, we have been made to be the children of the wisest, most loving Father that the universe has ever known. He is never, ever confused. He knows our every need because he created us. We can rest in the grace that has made us his children, knowing that our place in his family guarantees that we will have what we need.

FOR FURTHER STUDY AND ENCOURAGEMENT
Psalm 145

DAY 26

Your rest is not to be found in figuring your life out, but in trusting the one who has it all figured out for your good and his glory.

WE WERE IN THE CAR with our two young boys when the three-year-old asked out of the blue, "Daddy, if God made everything, did he make light poles?" I had the thought that all parents have, again and again, as they deal with the endless "why" questions that little ones ask: "How do we get from where we are to where we need to be in this conversation?" Or, "Why does he have to ask me 'why' questions all the time?"

Human beings have a deep desire to know and understand. We spend much of our daily mental time trying to figure things out. We don't live by instinct. We don't leave our lives alone. We are all theologians. We are all philosophers. We are all archaeologists who dig into the mounds of our lives to try to make sense of the civilization that is our story. This God-designed mental motivation is accompanied by wonderful and mysterious analytical gifts. This drive and those gifts set us apart from the rest of creation. They are holy, created by God to draw us to him, so that we can know him and understand ourselves in light of his existence and will.

But sin makes this drive and these gifts dangerous. They tempt us to think that we can find our hearts by figuring it all out. It's the "If only I could understand this or that, then I'd be secure" way of living. But it never works. In your most brilliant moment, you will still be left with mystery in your life; sometimes even painful mystery. We all face things that appear to make little sense and don't seem to serve any good purpose. So rest is never found in the quest to understand it all. No, rest is found in trusting the one who understands it all and rules it all for his glory and our good.

Few passages capture that rest better than Psalm 62:5–7: "For God alone, O my soul, wait in silence, for my hope is from him. He only is my rock and my salvation, my fortress; I shall not be shaken. On God rests my salvation and my glory; my mighty rock, my refuge is God."

In moments when you wish you knew what you can't know, there is rest to be found. There is one who knows. He loves you and rules what you don't understand with your good in mind.

FOR FURTHER STUDY AND ENCOURAGEMENT

2 Corinthians 5:1–10

DAY 27

*Today you'll encounter things that will
confuse you, but rest assured the one who
rules all those things is not confused.*

WE REALLY DON'T KNOW MUCH. Every day we are all greeted with mysteries. None of us can predict for sure where our personal stories are going. We are all confused about what happens to us, to those close to us, and in the world in which we live. As much as we try to make sense of our lives, there are things that we simply aren't able to understand. Here's what all of this means—you and I will never find inner peace and rest by trying to figure it all out. Peace is found in resting in the wisdom and grace of the one who has it all figured out and rules it all for his glory and our good.

When our children were very young, when I would refuse to let them do something, they didn't understand why, so they would begin to protest. I would then get down on my knees so we could be face to face, and then I would talk with them. The conversation would go like this:

"Do you know that your daddy loves you?"

"Yes, I know my daddy loves me."

"Is your daddy mean and bad to you?"

"No, you don't like to be mean."

"Is your daddy a horrible, bad daddy?"

"No."

"Then listen to what daddy is going to say. I would like to
why I had to say 'no' to what you wanted to do, but I

can't. If I explained it to you, you wouldn't understand anyway, so here's what you need to do. You need to walk down the hallway and say to yourself, 'I don't know why daddy said no to me, but I know my daddy loves me and I'm going to trust my daddy.' I really do love you."

"I love you too."

There is so much that we don't understand. There is so much that we are incapable of understanding. So rest is found in trusting the Father. He is not confused, and he surely does have your best interest in mind. Yes, he will ask you to do hard things and he will bring difficult things your way, but he is worthy of your trust and he loves you dearly. Today your heavenly Father reaches down to you and says: "I know you don't understand all that you face, but remember, I love you. Trust me and you will find peace that can be found no other way."

FOR FURTHER STUDY AND ENCOURAGEMENT
Isaiah 40:1–11

DAY 28

You don't have to understand everything in your life,
because your Lord of wisdom and grace understands it all.

IT IS A PARADOX THAT MANY of us don't handle well. We were created by God to be rational human beings and we carry around with us a desire to know and understand, but we must not forget that we will never experience inner peace simply because all our questions have been answered. Biblical faith is not irrational, but it takes us beyond our ability to reason. As believers in our identity as God's image-bearers and the truthfulness of his word, we do recognize that it is important to study, to learn, to examine, to evaluate, and to know. But we are not rationalists. We do not trust our reason more than we trust God. We do not reject what God says is true when it doesn't make sense to us, and we know that God's secret will leaves us with mysteries in our lives; mysteries that, even with the best of our theology, we won't be able to solve. Biblical literacy does not dispel all confusion and mystery from your life because while God reveals his will for you in the Bible, he does not reveal all the things he will do in your life for your good and his glory. God surprises you.

So you ask, "Where is peace to be found?" This question is answered clearly and powerfully in Isaiah 26:

> You keep him in perfect peace
>   whose mind is stayed on you,
>   because he trusts in you.

Trust in the LORD forever,
for the LORD God is an everlasting rock. (vv. 3–4)

This passage tells us where peace is to be found. It is never found in trying to figure out the secret will of God. It's not to be found in personal planning or attempts to control the circumstances and people in your life. Peace is found in trusting the person who controls all the things that you don't understand and who knows no mystery because he has planned it all. How do you experience this remarkable peace—the kind of peace that doesn't fade away when disappointments come, when people are difficult, or when circumstances are hard? You experience it by keeping your mind stayed on the Lord. The more you meditate on his glory, his power, his wisdom, his grace, his faithfulness, his righteousness, his patience, his zeal to redeem, and his commitment to his eternal promises to you, the more you can deal with mystery in your life. Why? Because you know the one behind the mystery is gloriously good, worthy not only of your trust but also the worship of your heart. It really is true that peace in times of trouble is not found in figuring out your life, but in worship of the one who has everything figured out already.

FOR FURTHER STUDY AND ENCOURAGEMENT

Psalm 139

DAY 29

*Discouragement focuses more on the broken glories
of creation than it does on the restoring glories
of God's character, presence, and promises.*

THEY WERE STANDING ON THE borders of the land that God had promised them. It stretched out with beauty before their eyes. They had sent explorers into the land to check it out. The report came back that it was rich and lush, producing sweet and succulent fruit. But the children of Israel were not jumping up and down in celebration and anticipation. They were not champing at the bit to get going. They were doing quite the opposite; they were digging in their heels and refusing to move at all. They stood there grumbling against the Lord, saying: "Because the LORD hated us he has brought us out of the land of Egypt, to give us into the hands of the Amorites, to destroy us. . . . 'The people are greater and taller than we. The cities are great and fortified up to heaven'" (Deut. 1:27–28).

The Bible says that these historical moments, significant times of spiritual evaluation and decision, have been recorded for our example and our instruction because these were people just like us. It was the most wonderful moment of grace in their lives. They were about to be given what they did not deserve and could not earn. Life, rich and full, was on the other side of that border. It was theirs for the taking because the one who had redeemed them from bondage was not just a deliverer of freedom; he was also a giver of life. They had earned nothing, but they were about to get it all. But they refused. They would not move. It all seemed unrealistic and impossible. It seemed like a cruel setup; the big, spiritual bait and switch. They had been promised a land of their own, but what they were getting was a place filled with people who didn't want them there. What in the world was God doing anyway?

Their disappointed thinking had a fatal flaw in it. What they saw as being in the way of God's plan was actually part of his plan; what caused their faith to weaken was actually God's tool to build their faith.

God knows what you too are facing. He sees well the brokenness that is all around you. He is not in a panic, wondering how he'll ever pull off his plan with all these obstacles in the way. Don't be discouraged. God has you exactly where he wants you. He knows just how he will use what makes you afraid in order to build your faith. He is not surprised by the troubles you face, and he surely has no intention of leaving you to face those things on your own. He stands with you in power, glory, goodness, wisdom, and grace. He can defeat what you can't, and he intends these troubles to be not enemies that finish you but tools of grace that transform you.

FOR FURTHER STUDY AND ENCOURAGEMENT

Joshua 1

DAY 30

*Does discouragement preach to you a false gospel
that causes you to forget that your future has already
been written into the pages of God's book?*

IT IS DISCOURAGING TO FACE

- your struggle with sin
- the disloyalty of a friend
- the rebellion of your children
- the souring of your marriage
- the division of your church
- the temptations that seem to be all around you
- the injustice that lives in this fallen world
- the pain and worry of physical sickness
- the loss of your job
- the hardship of old age
- the death of your dreams

Yes, it's hard to face all of these things. It's easy to lose your way. It's tempting to wonder what God is doing, if he cares, and if he hears your prayers. It's hard to hold on to his promises. It's hard to stay committed to good spiritual habits. It's hard not to give in to discouragement and give way to the desire to quit.

But in the face of discouragement, there is one thing that you need to remember. It is captured in just a few powerful words from Psalm 139: "Your eyes saw my unformed substance; in your book were written, every one of them, the days that were formed for me, when as yet there were none of them" (v. 16). It is vital to remember, when trouble comes your way and discouragement begins to grip your heart, that every single day of your life was written into God's book before you lived the very first of them. None of those days and none of the things that you have faced or will face in those days are a surprise to your Lord. He carefully authored the content of every one of those days with his own hand. He controlled every twist and turn of the plot that is your story. He introduced all the characters and determined all of the locations. Nothing will happen to you that he has not written into his book. And he has already determined how your story will end.

You see, what discourages you doesn't surprise him because he authored it all with a glorious combination of wisdom and grace. Nothing is out of his control. Your Savior is sovereign. He knows what is best and will do what is best. This is where rest and courage are to be found when discouragement shakes the resolve of your heart.

FOR FURTHER STUDY AND ENCOURAGEMENT

Psalm 135

DAY 31

*Don't be discouraged today. Yes, you're aware
of your weaknesses and failures, but for each of
them there's forgiving, transforming grace.*

WHEN YOU READ IT, it doesn't seem right. It seems that you've entered some topsy-turvy, inside-out universe. But Paul is both serious and dead right in what he says:

> So to keep me from becoming conceited because of the surpassing greatness of the revelations, a thorn was given me in the flesh, a messenger of Satan to harass me, to keep me from becoming conceited. Three times I pleaded with the Lord about this, that it should leave me. But he said to me, "My grace is sufficient for you, for my power is made perfect in weakness." Therefore I will boast all the more gladly of my weaknesses, so that the power of Christ may rest upon me. For the sake of Christ, then, I am content with weaknesses, insults, hardships, persecutions, and calamities. For when I am weak, then I am strong. (2 Cor. 12:7–10)

Fasten your seat belts; here we go. God chooses for you to be weak to protect you from you and to cause you to value the strength that only he can give. In this way, the weaknesses that he sends our way are not impediments to the good life. They are not in the way of his loving plan. They are not signs of his lack of care. They are not indicators of the failure of his promises. They do not expose gaps in the theology that we hold dear. They are not indications that the Bible contradicts itself when it says that God will meet all of your needs. No, these weaknesses are tools of his zealous and amazing grace. They protect you from the arrogance of self-reliance that tempts us all. They keep you from thinking that you're capable of what you're not. They remind you that you are needy and were created to be dependent on one greater than you. They cause you to do what all of us in some way resist doing—humbly run to God in faith for the help that only he can give.

So your weaknesses are not the big danger that you should fear. What you should really fear are your delusions of strength. When you tell yourself that you are strong, you quit being excited about God's rescuing, transforming, and empowering grace. Paul actually celebrated his weaknesses, because as he did, the power of God rested upon him. He didn't live a fearful, discouraged, and envious life; he was content because he knew weakness is the doorway to real power, power that only God can and willingly does supply.

FOR FURTHER STUDY AND ENCOURAGEMENT
Ephesians 6:10–20

DAY 32

*You don't have to be anxious about the
future. A God of grace has invaded your life,
and he always completes what he starts.*

IT'S NATURAL; WE ALL DO IT. We all wonder about what is to
come. Some of us think about the future and hope our dreams
will come true. Some of us dread the future and pray that we
will not have to face the things that we fear. For some of us, the
future seems foggy and unknowable. For all of us, it's hard to
look into the future and be secure, because the future is simply
out of our hands. With all of our consideration, meditation,
and planning for what is to come, things never turn out the
way we envisioned. There are always unexpected turns in the
road. There are potholes and ditches we did not anticipate.
There are mountains and valleys we just did not foresee. We
find ourselves walking through moments of darkness when we
thought we'd be living and walking in the light. It doesn't take
long for us to begin to acquiesce to the fact that we don't ever
quite know what is around the next corner.

But we don't have to live plagued by the anxiety of the
unknown. We don't have to go to sleep wondering what the
next day will bring or wake up working our way through all
the "what-ifs" we can think of. We don't have to seek some
means to figure out what we will never be able to figure out.
No, we can have rest when we are confused. We can experience peace in the face of the unknown. We can feel an inner

well-being while living in the middle of mystery. Why? Because our peace of heart does not rest on how much we know, how much we have figured out, or how accurately we have been able to predict the future. No, our rest is in the person who holds our individual futures in his wise and gracious hands. We have peace because we know that he will complete the good things that he in grace has initiated in our lives. He is faithful, so he never leaves the work of his hands. He is gracious, so he gives us what we need, not what we deserve. He is wise, so what he does is always best. He is sovereign, so he rules all the situations and locations where we live. He is powerful, so he can do what he pleases, when he pleases.

Paul says it well in Philippians 1:6: "And I am sure of this, that he who began a good work in you will bring it to completion at the day of Jesus Christ." Are you experiencing anxiety because you've forgotten who you are and what you've been given? Are you experiencing the fear that results from trying to know what you'll never know? He knows, he cares, and he will complete the job he's begun.

FOR FURTHER STUDY AND ENCOURAGEMENT
Romans 8:18–39

DAY 33

*If God is in control of every aspect of your
world and his grace covers all your sin,
why would you ever give way to fear?*

THERE ARE MANY THINGS I WISH were true about me:

I wish I could say that I'm never afraid, but I can't.

I wish I could say that worry never interrupts my sleep, but I can't.

I wish I could say that I never wonder what God is doing, but I can't.

I wish I could say that I never give way to envy, but I can't.

I wish I could say that I am always aware that God is near, but I can't.

I wish I could say that I never wonder, "If only_____," but I can't.

I wish I could say that I never dread what's around the corner, but I can't.

I wish I could say that I always have peace in my heart, but I can't.

I wish I could say that all that I do is done out of faith and not fear, but I can't.

You see, I have come to be very aware that although I know the Bible and its doctrine well, the battle between fear and faith still goes on in my heart. Here's what this means at street level. It is important to understand why fear still lives in the life of a believer in the hallways, kitchens, bedrooms, family rooms, workrooms, and vans of everyday life. You could argue that he or she has every reason to be free of fear, that fear should be an artifact of a former civilization. So why the continued struggle with fear?

Fear lives and rules in the heart of a believer who has forgotten God's sovereignty and grace. If left to myself, I *should* be afraid. There are many trials, temptations, dangers, and enemies in this fallen world that are bigger and more powerful than me. I have to deal with many things that are outside my control. But the message of the gospel is that I haven't been left to myself, that Immanuel is with me in sovereign authority and powerful grace. He rules with perfect wisdom over all the circumstances and locations that would make me afraid. In grace, he blesses me with what I need to face what he has decided to put on my plate. I am never—in anything, anywhere, at any time—by myself. I never arrive on the scene first. I never step into a situation that exists outside his control. I never move beyond the reach of his authority. He is never surprised by where I end up or by what I am facing. He never leaves me to the limited resources of my own wisdom, strength, and righteousness. He never grows weary with protecting and providing for me. He will never abandon me out of frustration. I do not need to be afraid. When you forget God's sovereignty and his grace, you give room in your heart for fear to do its nasty, debilitating work. Pray right now for grace to remember. Your sovereign Savior loves to hear and answer.

FOR FURTHER STUDY AND ENCOURAGEMENT
Isaiah 44:1–8

DAY 34

*You don't have to worry about whether your
world is under control. God rules. You just have to
learn to trust him when his rule isn't evident.*

I LOOKED EVERYWHERE. I looked high and low. There wasn't
a drawer, a cabinet, or a dark closet I didn't tear apart in my
search. I even went out to the car twice to make sure I hadn't
left it there. The file contained important papers, and I had
lost it somewhere. It was so frustrating. And after all my searching, it was just as lost as when I had begun. That night it hit
me that my lost file was a picture of how little control I have
over my own life. I do not even have sovereignty over my little
world to guarantee that I will never lose important things. It
can be a bit scary to consider. You and I have very little power
and control over the most significant things in our lives. You
and I don't know what's going to happen next. We don't have
a clue what will be on our plates next week or next month.
We have little control over the principal people in our lives,
little power over the situations in which we live, and almost
no control over the locations of our lives.

Honestly facing your lack of sovereignty over your own life
produces either anxiety or relief. Anxiety is God-forgetting.
It is the result of thinking that life is on your shoulders, that
it is your job to figure it all out and keep things in order. It's
worrisome to think that your job in life is to work yourself
into enough control over people, locations, and situations that

you can rest assured that you will get what you think you need and accomplish what you think you need to accomplish. If you fall into this way of thinking, your life will be burdened with worry and your heart will be filled with dread.

But there is a much better way. It is God-remembering. It rests in the relief that although it may not look like it, your life is under the careful control of one who defines wisdom, power, and love. In all of those moments when life is out of *your* control, it is not out of *his* control: "For his dominion is an everlasting dominion, and his kingdom endures from generation to generation; . . . and he does according to his will among the host of heaven and among the inhabitants of the earth; and none can stay his hand or say to him, 'What have you done?'" (Dan. 4:34–35).

You see, rest is not to be found in your control but in God's absolute rule over everything. You will never be in a situation, location, or relationship that is not under his control.

FOR FURTHER STUDY AND ENCOURAGEMENT

Psalm 97

DAY 35

Mercy means I am so deeply grateful for the forgiveness I
have received that I cannot help offering you the same.

WE ALL DO IT, PROBABLY EVERY DAY. We have no idea that we're
doing it, yet it has a huge impact on the way we view ourselves
and the way we respond to others. It is one of the reasons there
is so much relational trouble even in the house of God. What
is this thing that we all tend to do that causes so much harm?
We all forget. In the busyness and self-centeredness of our lives,
we sadly forget how much our lives have been blessed by and
radically redirected by mercy. The fact that God has blessed
us with his favor when we deserved his wrath fades from our
memories like a song whose lyrics we once knew but now cannot recall. The reality that on every morning brand-new mercy
greets us is not the thing that grips our minds as we frenetically
prepare for our day. When we lay our exhausted heads down
at the end of the day for much-needed sleep, we often fail
to look back on the many mercies that dripped from God's
hands onto our little lives. We don't often take time to sit and
meditate on what our lives would've been like if the mercy of
the Redeemer had not been written into our personal stories.
Sadly, we all tend to be way too mercy forgetful.

Mercy forgetfulness is dangerous, because it shapes the way
you think about yourself and others. When you remember
mercy, you also remember that you simply did nothing whatsoever to earn that with which mercy has blessed you. When

you remember mercy, you are humble, thankful, and tender. When you remember mercy, complaining gives way to gratitude and self-focused desire gives way to worship. But when you forget mercy, you proudly tell yourself that what you have is what you've achieved. When you forget mercy, you take credit for what only mercy could produce. When you forget mercy, you name yourself as righteous and deserving, and you live an entitled and demanding life.

When you forget mercy and think you're deserving, you find it all too easy not to extend mercy to others. Proudly, you think that you're getting what you deserve and that they are, too. Your proud heart is not tender, so it is not easily moved by the sorry plight of others. You forget that you are more like than unlike your needy brother, failing to acknowledge that neither of you stands before God as deserving. Humility is the soil in which mercy for others grows. Gratitude for mercy given is what motivates mercy extended. Paul says, "Be kind to one another, tenderhearted, forgiving one another, as God in Christ forgave you" (Eph. 4:32).

FOR FURTHER STUDY AND ENCOURAGEMENT
Luke 6:27–36; Matthew 18:21–35

DAY 36

When you're weary with the battle, remember that the one who is your strength never takes a break, never needs sleep, never grows weary.

LIFE IN THIS FALLEN WORLD is wearisome. Sometimes your marriage is just exhausting as you work to make a sinner married to a sinner coexist in love and peace. Sometimes it's just plain tiring to be a parent, particularly on those days when it seems that your children have conspired together to be corporately rebellious. Sometimes you don't feel like being nice to that neighbor who seems to be able to look at everything and find a reason to complain. Sometimes you just get exhausted with dealing with your heart—you know, those desires you shouldn't have and those thoughts you shouldn't think. Sometimes you have to drag yourself to your church service or your small group. Sometimes you'd just like to get off the Christianity treadmill and zone out, but you can't. You wake up the next day and you have to do it all over again—another temptation, another marital misunderstanding, another conflict with another friend, another resistant child, or another moment when you feel the emotional temperature change.

When you're weary and feeling weak, run to the Psalms; there's grace to be found there:

I lift up my eyes to the hills.
    From where does my help come?
My help comes from the LORD,

who made heaven and earth.
He will not let your foot be moved;
   he who keeps you will not slumber.
Behold, he who keeps Israel
   will neither slumber nor sleep.
The Lord is your keeper;
   the Lord is your shade on your right hand.
The sun shall not strike you by day,
   nor the moon by night.
The Lord will keep you from all evil;
   he will keep your life.
The Lord will keep
   your going out and your coming in
   from this time forth and forevermore. (Ps. 121)

This psalm confronts you and me with two truths that we must always remember. First, we are not in this battle alone. We have a keeper, and our safety is his commitment. Second, the one who is our keeper never, ever takes a break. His keeping care is 24/7 forever and ever. The inexhaustible keeper is your help and strength; when weary, run to him in faith.

FOR FURTHER STUDY AND ENCOURAGEMENT
Psalm 91

DAY 37

*Waiting on God doesn't mean sitting around and
hoping. Waiting means believing he will do what
he's promised and then acting with confidence.*

WAITING ON GOD IS NOT at all like the meaningless waiting that
you do at the dentist's office. You know, he's overbooked, so
you're still sitting there more than an hour past your scheduled
appointment. You're a man, but you're now reading *Family
Circle* magazine. You've begun to read the article titled "The
7 Best Chicken Recipes in the World." When you're a man
and you're getting ready to tear a chicken recipe out of *Family
Circle* magazine because the recipe sounds so good, you know
that you have been waiting too long!

But waiting on God is not like that. Waiting on God is an
active life based on confidence in his presence and promises,
not a passive existence haunted by occasional doubt. Waiting
on God isn't internal torment that results in paralysis. No, waiting on God is internal rest that results in courageous action.

Waiting is your calling. Waiting is your blessing. Every one
of God's children has been chosen to wait, because every one
of God's children lives between the "already" and the "not yet."
Already this world has been broken by sin, but not yet has it
been made new again. Already Jesus has come, but not yet has
he returned to take you home with him forever. Already your
sin has been forgiven, but not yet have you been fully delivered
from it. Already Jesus reigns, but not yet has his final kingdom

come. Already sin has been defeated, but not yet has it been completely destroyed. Already the Holy Spirit has been given, but not yet have you been perfectly formed into the likeness of Jesus. Already God has given you his word, but not yet has it totally transformed your life. Already you have been given grace, but not yet has that grace finished its work. You see, we're all called to wait because we all live right smack dab in the middle of God's grand redemptive story. We all wait for the final end of the work that God has begun in and for us.

We don't just wait—we wait in hope. And what does hope in God look like? It is a confident expectation of a guaranteed result. We wait believing that what God has begun he will complete, so we live with confidence and courage. We get up every morning and act upon what is to come, and because what is to come is sure, we know that our labor in God's name is never in vain. So we wait and act. We wait and work. We wait and fight. We wait and conquer. We wait and proclaim. We wait and run. We wait and sacrifice. We wait and give. We wait and worship. Waiting on God is an action based on confident assurance of grace to come.

FOR FURTHER STUDY AND ENCOURAGEMENT

Romans 4

DAY 38

*Faith is living in light of what God has said, resting in
what he has done, and entrusting the future to his care.*

IT IS AN INCREDIBLE STORY, a clear case study in what faith is
and does:

> By faith Abraham, when he was tested, offered up Isaac,
> and he who had received the promises was in the act of
> offering up his only son, of whom it was said, "Through
> Isaac shall your offspring be named." He considered that
> God was able even to raise him from the dead, from
> which, figuratively speaking, he did receive him back.
> (Heb. 11:17–19)

God had promised Abraham that his descendants would be
like the stars in the sky and that through his descendants all
the nations of the earth would be blessed. But Abraham and
his wife, Sarah, didn't have any children, let alone a clue about
how he would pass down the promise to the next generation.
They waited and waited. Decade piled up on decade, but no
son came. Abraham was an old man, and Sarah was decades
beyond her childbearing years. Then, in a miracle of God's
faithfulness, a son, Isaac, was born. There must have been some
kind of celebration that day! God was true to his promises. He
did have the power to deliver. He would keep his covenant.
Blessing would come to this sin-broken world. It seemed like
the end of a beautiful story.

Then God came to Abraham and told him to sacrifice the promised son! It made no sense whatsoever. All God's promises of faithfulness and all the hopes of his covenant rested on this boy. If Abraham killed him, it would all be over. If Isaac died, nothing that had happened for decades would make any sense. You can imagine Abraham saying: "God, ask anything of me, but not this; please, not this. You promised me a son. I waited in faith, and now you want me to kill him. God, I just don't understand." We don't know all the emotions that were inside Abraham, but there is little hint of angst and anger in his reactions. Abraham immediately began to prepare to do what God had called him to do. We know that grace had visited and transformed the heart of this man, or he would not have been able to react as he did.

It's clear that Abraham did not know why God was asking him to do what he had asked, and it is clear that he did not know what God was going to do. Abraham reasoned that maybe God would resurrect Isaac after the sacrifice, but that was not what God was intending. This is where this passage exposes what faith is about. Abraham wasn't relying on what he could see or understand. No, he was at rest because he acted on the firm platform of God's commands, as well as his presence, promises, faithfulness, and power. Faith believes that God really does exist and that he rewards those who seek him. But faith isn't natural for us; it is ours only as a gift of God's grace. Seek that grace again today.

FOR FURTHER STUDY AND ENCOURAGEMENT

Genesis 22

DAY 39

Don't buy the false gospel of self-reliance.
If you could make it without help,
Jesus would not have needed to come.

IT IS A SEDUCTIVE LIE. It's told again and again. There is nothing new in its message. It was told first in the garden of Eden and hasn't ceased to be told since. It is told in many forms:

- "No one knows you better than you know yourself."
- "You really don't need the ministry of others in your life."
- "You used to struggle with sin, but not anymore."
- "Since you know the Bible so well, you're probably okay."
- "Look at your track record; you've come a long way."
- "Your little sins aren't really that sinful."
- "You're way beyond the level where you need to be taught by others."
- "You're on your own; you just have to get up and do what you've been called to do."

The voices of self-reliance are many and deceptive. In some way, they greet you every day. Their deceptive whispers started in the garden and continue with the sole devious purpose of convincing you to rely on yourself and not on God. The lie of self-sufficiency is attractive to us all because we don't like to think of ourselves as weak and needy. We don't like to think of ourselves as dependent. We don't like to think of ourselves as fools who need to be rescued from ourselves. We like the story of the self-made man; you know, the person who pulled himself out of the mire and made it on his own with no one to thank but himself.

But the message of the gospel is devastatingly humbling. It tells me that I am in a hopeless, impossible, and irreversible state apart from divine intervention. Even Adam and Eve could not make it on their own. Even though they were perfect people living in a perfect world and in a perfect relationship with God, they did not have the ability to go it alone. So immediately after creating them, God began to give them his revelation, because he knew they would not figure life out on their own. They were dependent on the words of God in order to make proper sense out of life. They could not be what they were supposed to be and do what they were supposed to do without God's counsel and his help. Now, that was the state of people before sin entered the world and did its internal and external damage. How much more is it true of us!

Self-reliance is a lie that leads you nowhere good. You do not have what you need inside yourself to live as you were created to live. So a God of tender grace comes to you in the person of his Son and offers you everything you need for life and godliness. In grace, he is ever with you because he knows you'll never make it on your own.

FOR FURTHER STUDY AND ENCOURAGEMENT
John 6:60–65

DAY 40

When nothing else or no one else in your life remains and is faithful, you can rest assured that God will be both.

I LOVE THE HONESTY OF THE BIBLE. I love that faith in God doesn't require you and me to play monkey games with reality. I love that the Bible's description of life in this fallen world is accurate and familiar. Psalm 90 is one of the most honest and descriptive psalms. How's this for honesty? "The years of our life are seventy, or even by reason of strength eighty; yet their span is but toil and trouble; they are soon gone, and we fly away" (v. 10). Here's what the psalmist is saying: "Your life will be short and will be marked by difficulty." Not very good news is it? But it's true. You live in a fallen world that itself groans, waiting for redemption. You live with flawed people who think, say, and do wrong things. You live in a place where corruption, immorality, injustice, pollution, and disease still live and do their ugly work. You live in an environment that does not function according to God's original design. Every day is marked by little troubles, and big troubles will enter your door as well.

In all this, you are tempted to feel alone, forsaken, poor, and unable. In all this, you are tempted to wonder whether God exists, let alone if he hears or cares. In your trouble, some people around you are insensitive and unloving. They find your troubles to be too much of a burden. And the people who are sensitive and loving have little power to erase your trouble. This is why the beginning of this psalm of trouble is so important. This honest psalm doesn't begin with trouble; it begins with the most important declaration that anyone who faces trouble could ever hear: "Lord, you have been our dwelling place in all generations. Before the mountains were brought forth, or ever you had formed the earth and the world, from everlasting to everlasting you are God" (vv. 1–2).

If you are God's child, you are not alone. Glorious grace has connected you by faith to the one whose power and love don't shift with the times. Grace has connected you and me to the one who is the ultimate dwelling place, the ultimate place to which we can run. This means that I am never left just to my own resources. I am never left to figure out and deal with life on my own. As God's child, I must never see myself as poor or forsaken. I must never buy into the lie that I have no recourse or hope. I must never think that my life is ruled by my difficulty. I must never give way to despondency or despair. Grace has opened the door of hope and refuge to me by connecting me to one who is eternal and who rules all the circumstances and relationships that would cause me to feel alone.

FOR FURTHER STUDY AND ENCOURAGEMENT
Psalm 86

SCRIPTURE INDEX

PAUL TRIPP MINISTRIES

Paul Tripp Ministries is a not-for-profit organization connecting the transforming power of Jesus Christ to everyday life. Hundreds of resources are freely available online, on social media, and the Paul Tripp app.

PaulTripp.com

 /pdtripp   @paultripp   @paultrippquotes

More Devotionals
from Paul David Tripp

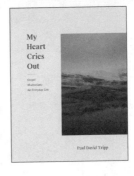

For more information, visit **crossway.org, paultripp.com,**
or anywhere Christian books are sold.